St. Marys c/o R.W.

SY 0033106 6

ST MARY'S COLLEGE LIBRARY FALLS ROAD

J/919.4 GRI 62215

D0244274

Kids Oz

An Introduction to Australia

Warrill Grindrod and Dan Gardiner

CONTENTS

OZ AHOY!

SYDNEYSIDERS

Sydney is a city on the water. It spreads round a large bay with low cliffs and little beaches. Bondi Beach is one which faces the open sea. Dalia and Nikki live at Bondi Beach. They are eleven years old.

Like most Sydneysiders, Dalia and Nikki love to go swimming and surfing. Even their school is at the beach! (See page 62)

> 'In Sydney we've got the Harbour Bridge, the Opera House and Centre Point Tower, and on my verandah you can see all the lights at night-time. It looks really good.'
> *Nikki*

Dalia and Nikki are proud of their beautiful city, with its immense harbour and its 'coat-hanger'. (Can you see why the bridge is called a coat-hanger?) Look for the strange shell-like Opera House nearby, and for the high-rise offices and the television tower in the centre.

The bridge takes non-stop traffic from north to south, but you need other transport around the shores. Can you see the ferries, which zig-zag across the bay, taking Sydneysiders to work? They even take children to school. How would you like a boat trip every day?

Did You Know?

- Nearly 16 million people live in Australia, and about 14 million of them live in towns and cities.
- Sydney is Australia's largest city (3.5 million people).
- Sydney covers about the same area as Greater London but has half as many people.
- The main span of Sydney Harbour Bridge is 503 metres long.
- Sydney Tower is the tallest building in the southern hemisphere (325 metres).

Two lovers met on Sydney Bridge,
Their lips were all a-tingle.
He kissed her and her teeth fell out
And now the lady's single!

KOORIES, ANANGU AND NYOONGAHS

There were people living in Australia long before the Europeans arrived. We call them the Aboriginal People. ('Aboriginal' simply means 'from the beginning'.) They lived across the whole continent and knew how to live even in the deserts. Many still do.

In south-eastern Australia the Aboriginal word for 'people' is Koorie. In central Australia it is Anangu, and around Perth, Nyoongah. The different peoples are divided into many different 'tribes', each with its own name.

Nowadays, most Aboriginal People have been moved off their tribal lands and live on the edges of towns and cities. As you read this book, you'll begin to understand why so many of them are poor.

Gordon, Crystal and Sally are ten years old. They are Nyoongah children living on the outskirts of Perth. Their elders teach them some of the old ways:

'We Nyoongahs believe that the earth, the animals, and we ourselves, are all part of the same beginning, the Dreamtime. The land is our mother, and its waterholes, rocks, trees and rivers were formed by our ancestors. They were spirits. This is why the land and its animals are very special and sacred for us, like the churches or temples of other peoples.'

'Because life is often hard, Nyoongahs look after each other. Sharing is important to us, and so are our ceremonies and celebrations. The Corroboree is a tribal dance. In one dance, we celebrate the spearing of a crocodile.'

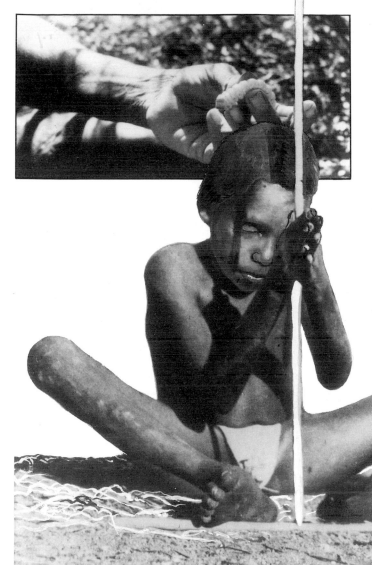

'You, Crystal and Sally, would help to gather food in woven dilly bags. We women often provided more for the tribe than the men. Near the sea we collected shellfish. Inland, we found lizards, honey-ants, roots and yams. A very special food for us was the wichetty grub.

'Each of our tribes kept on the move, otherwise the food supply would run out. We burnt the land before moving on. This cleared the scrub, fertilised the soil, and helped food plants to grow. When we stayed in one place for a while, we made shelters from branches.

'Nyoongah children learn how to make fire, by twirling a long pointed stick against a piece of softwood until it heats up and sets fire to dry leaves and sticks.'

Aboriginal words	
(from different tribes)	
eugaries	*shellfish*
billah	*spear*
chulaggie	*bird*
billabong	*pool*
wollunqua	*snake*
pirla-pirla	*baby*
worrin	*sun*
mia-mia	*shelter*

'You, Gordon, would learn to throw a spear a very long way, using a special spear-throwing stick called a woomera. To catch birds, you would learn to throw a boomerang and whirl it into a flock overhead.

'The boomerang is a specially curved piece of wood. It works a bit like a propeller, lifting itself into the air as it whirls round. Some boomerangs return to the person who throws them. Carving boomerangs is a very skilled job.

'Although animals are part of the creation, our people could hunt and fish to eat, so long as they didn't kill for sport. Boys learnt from their fathers how to hunt kangaroos, emus, turtles and other animals.'

'The kangaroos have got to be killed the proper way. If you see six kangaroos over there, and you only need two, then you kill two. That's for tucker, the food you eat.'
Robert Bropho

'Tomorrow we will follow the Rainbow Serpent's law of regrowth by burning the grass land. In this way, when we come back, the grass will be sweet and the young wallabies will stay and eat. The seeds we throw will have grown into tall bushes bearing fruit and we will have a big feast.'
Vivian Walker

These are some of the things that Gordon, Crystal and Sally learn. Above all, they learn about living out in the open.

Changeless Australia

'When I first came here, I used to like looking at the clear skies and bright stars – especially because, well, it used to be pretty cloudy in England, eh? – didn't it!'
Jenny Balzer, originally from Bradford, Yorkshire

BBQ

BBQ

Nikki, Robert and David Campbell
invites
to A birthday BBQ
on Saturday 2nd January
at Bronte Beach
from 5 o'clock
P.S bring your boogie board and your
Scottish cousins

Australia does get cloudy skies and rain, but more often there are endless hours of sunshine. The weather makes you want to live and eat outside.

An invitation to a BBQ! What's that? If you don't know, then go expecting grilled steak, chops and sausages, with bread rolls, coleslaw and plenty to drink, because BBQ means barbecue. (And what's a boogie-board? Find out on page 62!)

Barbecues are all part of living outside. Who wants to slave over a hot kitchen stove when you can cook outside and get a tan as well?

A barbie is good at any time, for lunch or for tea. You can have one in your back yard, by your pool if you've got one, or down at the beach. City parks have barbecue areas with electric hotplates. You put a twenty-cent piece in the slot, and start cooking!

Bert's Pav Recipe

This is a giant cream meringue. A chef, Bert Sachse, made the first pavlova in Perth in 1935 and named it after the famous Russian ballerina, Anna Pavlova. You make it at home and take it out to eat after your steak and chops.

Ingredients

4 egg whites	1 teaspoon white vinegar
100 grams castor sugar	Vanilla
100 grams granulated sugar	Whipped cream
1 teaspoon cornflour	Fruit to decorate

1 Crack the eggs and separate the whites into a bowl. Whisk the whites as stiff as you can, until they stand up in little peaks.

2 Keep whisking and *slowly* add 100 grams of castor sugar and 100 grams of granulated sugar. Then sieve the cornflour over the mixture, and sprinkle the vinegar, and a few drops of vanilla over it as well. Gently fold in.

3 Spoon the mixture into a round heap on a baking tray covered with greaseproof paper. Make a large hollow in the middle.

4 Bake for two hours at a very low temperature in the bottom of the oven. The meringue is done when it's firm on the outside, and still a little bit soft and chewy in the middle. Turn off the oven and let the meringue cool.

5 Fill the middle of the meringue with whipped cream, and pile strawberries or kiwi fruit, or banana and passion fruit on top.

6 Now take your pav outside and grab your spoons.
Mmmmmmmmmmm!

Independent Kids

You have to grow up quickly in Australia, and learn to be independent, especially in the bush. Aussie mums and dads expect kids to lend a hand both inside and outside.

Adam and Sarah Litchfield live on a sheep station called Wilpoorinna in South Australia. Adam is nine and Sarah is seven. They do a lot around the property. They both work in the vegetable patch. If they didn't water it and spread manure on it, there wouldn't be any vegies.

You'll see more of their place later (on page 10).

> 'I often pick all the fruit, and since the garden is very very close to the chook-house, I do all the eggs. I haven't started pollinating the tomatoes yet . . . What we really need is some bees round here.'
>
> *Sarah*

You can enjoy yourself a lot in Australia, but you're expected to do your bit to help out. **No bludgers allowed!**

> 'A mob of fat cattle was on the road from Barclay tablelands to Adelaide in 1924. The drovers included a girl of fourteen years, from Helen Springs station, said to be the best hand with the mob.'
>
> *The Age*, 13 May 1924

INSIDE OUTSIDE

Inside, Australian homes aren't so very different from British homes. This is Sarah and Adam's kitchen at Wilpoorinna.

Outside, this is what the homestead looks like. The tank is very important. It collects rainwater for drinking. Most Australian houses in the bush and outback have tanks like this one.

The letterboxes are different too. They're not in the front door like British ones. They're at the front gate. And out in the bush, don't think you're close to the house when you see the letterbox, there could still be 5Ks to go! (Ks is what Aussies say for kilometres.)

The mail doesn't come very often (maybe once a week in the outback) so letterboxes need to be big. The letterbox also needs to keep out the weather because when it rains, it rains!

'It only rains once or twice a year. When it rains everybody goes crazy. They go out and sit in the rain.'
Ossie Balzer, Newman, Western Australia

Usually it's very dry in the outback, and that means there's hardly any grass, so some homes and schools have a grass pit for kids to play in – different from Britain's sandpits!

Coober Pedy is an opal-mining town in the outback. It's so hot there, that people live in underground homes called dugouts. If you go there on a visit you will find even the motel is a series of dugouts. It's not as bad as it sounds, and people make their dugouts as comfortable as homes above ground.

Australians love their homes to be comfortable and these days lots of them have swimming pools. But it wasn't always like this.

Did You Know?

- A settler is anybody who goes to live in a new land.
- A squatter is somebody who takes over a piece of land which doesn't belong to him, and claims it for his own property. In Australia, squatters claimed the best land and became rich.

The early settlers' houses were very simple because they had to make most of the things they needed from whatever materials were nearby. Things they couldn't make, like bathtubs, clothes and cooking pots, had to be imported from Britain and carried all the way into the bush. This made quite ordinary things very expensive.

Look at all the things this early squatter has used to try and make his hut comfortable.

CITY LIFE

Although Australians spend a lot of their spare time outside, they don't all live in the country. Most of them live in cities like Sydney, Melbourne, Brisbane and Perth.

You might have left Europe and come to Australia with your family a hundred years ago. Maybe you came from a gloomy city street in London or Manchester, and now you are expecting wide open spaces, and a new life. Imagine how you would have felt if your family had brought you to these cheap houses in Caraher's Lane in Sydney.

Caraher's Lane is in an area of Sydney called The Rocks. You can see The Rocks on the picture of modern Sydney on pages 2 and 3. It's just above the far end of the Harbour Bridge.

In those days, people probably felt that living in Sydney's slums was as bad as living in Europe.

People didn't have much money then. When the barrow boys came round, you hoped against hope they'd take pity on you, and give you a sweet or a lick of ice-cream. These days, you go to the milk bar – they sell everything!

Of course there were better-off parts of Sydney with wide streets and large houses.

Melbourne is really special because you can still ride on trams there. No other city in Australia has them (and nor do many in Europe or the USA). Most of the trams are green and cream, but some are decorated in wild and jazzy colours.

Tram tickets then and now

'When I go into the city I can't breathe properly because there's too much pollution from the cars.'
Mercedes Fernandez, Dalia's Mum

Australian cities are more cheerful nowadays. People wear colourful clothes, shops are bright, and there are all kinds of entertainments in the parks. As in most modern cities, there are plenty of new high-rise buildings, and many families, like Dalia's and Nikki's, live in flats.

'Living in Australia is still very confusing. Last month I went for a picnic with my brother. We lost each other in the afternoon. I looked for him for five hours and then I went back home. I didn't know what to do. My brother couldn't speak any English and he couldn't even read the signs. We found him the next day. He had caught the train to St Mary's.'
Cheng from Kampuchea

 is Fun!

Aussies take their sport seriously! It's an outdoor lifestyle with sporting activities from surfing to racing, cricket to windsurfing. Compared with Britain, far fewer kids have hobbies like model-making. The sun and the heat call you outside to sunbathe and enjoy yourself.

'Waterslides are sort of like a big slippery dip that's got water in it. It goes curving around and when you get to the end, all of a sudden you just go straight down like that, and you fly off. It's so scary – you don't know what's going to happen!'
Nikki and Robert, Sydney

Darwin's Beercan Regatta, kid-style – a Coke-can craft

The Snowy Mountains aren't so hot, but there's still fun-in-the-sun!

Oz is Festival!

January 26th, the end of the summer holidays, and boy it's hot! This is an important day, especially for British descendants. This is Australia Day, when Dalia and Nikki come with their parents to Macquarie Point in Sydney. They watch dressed-up soldiers and sailors re-enact the landing of the first settlers in 1788.

Nowadays people from all over the world come to live in Australia – Chinese, Italians, Greeks, Yugoslavs, Indians, Japanese, Vietnamese and many more.

> 'My mother and father are Spanish, my brother's Australian, and I'm Australian. Mum and Dad speak Spanish at home. I understand it, but I don't speak it.'
>
> *Dalia*

Kids go with their families to national festivals. For a little while, a street or a park in Australia can seem like a part of China or Spain.

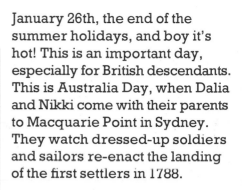

Did You Know?

- Melbourne is the second-largest Greek city in the world after Athens!

Corroboree time!

Chinese New Year celebrations

15

In 1783, John Hudson worked as a chimney-sweep in London. He was nine years old and an orphan. Mary Branham was a servant girl, a little older than John. They did not know each other yet, but they were fated to share some strange and terrible experiences.

Mary and John didn't get much fresh food because it had to be brought from the country in slow horse-drawn carts and cost too much. They were often shivering because wood and coal were so expensive. They couldn't afford good clothes or shoes, and they lived in unhealthy, cramped rooms or cellars with no toilets or running water. They might have shared a room with ten or twelve brothers and sisters. Most children caught diseases and didn't live very long. If John and Mary were lucky they would live until they were forty. Few people lived beyond fifty. All they could expect from life was hard work, not much to eat, and not much fun.

Because they were so poor and so hungry, John and Mary had to live by their wits. If you had lived then, you would have known that (even though you were a child) you could be hanged for stealing a sheep or a horse. John and Mary knew that.

Then of course it happened. They were caught, and sent to face trial. Imagine their thoughts as they lay down on the dirty straw bedding in a dark and crowded, smelly prison cell.

In spite of the punishments, the prisons were full. One way of emptying them was to send the prisoners, or convicts, overseas to work. This was called 'transportation'. In October 1783, John Hudson stood trembling in the dock at the Lord Mayor's court in London. The jury found him guilty of breaking and entering. The judge decided not to sentence John to hang because of his 'tender age'. He was sentenced to seven years' transportation instead.

> . . . John Hudson did burglariously and feloniously break and enter the dwelling house of William Holdsworth, at the hour of one in the night, on the 10th of October last, stealing one linen shirt, value 10s., five silk stockings, value 5s., one pistol, value 5s., and two aprons, value 2s . . .
> *Old Bailey Session Papers*, 1783

At about this time, Mary was also convicted of stealing and sentenced to transportation. She and John were both convicts now.

Many convicts were kept in the hulks of old ships, moored in the River Thames. Damp and foul, they were far worse than the city prisons. What would be on your mind if you were being rowed out to begin a sentence in one of these hulks?

The registers were full of prisoners' names, all waiting for transportation. At last, John and Mary's names came up. After spending three years in the hulks, John Hudson and Mary Branham were about to be transported to Botany Bay.

A New Transportation Colony

In 1770, Captain Cook charted the east coast of Australia, and named it New South Wales. He wasn't the first European to reach Australia. The Portuguese and the Dutch had landed on the west and south coasts, perhaps centuries earlier.

On board Captain Cook's ship was a naturalist, Joseph Banks. He was so fascinated by the range of plants in one of the bays along the coast, that he named it Botany Bay.

When he got back to London, Joseph Banks suggested this would be a very good place to start another colony for transportation, and in 1786 the British government agreed.

The First Fleet

In 1787, John Hudson and Mary Branham were taken to Portsmouth Harbour. John was thirteen now. He was lined up with all the other male convicts. They had to undress, and buckets of cold seawater were thrown over them, in case they had any diseases. When all the jail-dirt was washed off, they were given new clothes. Mary Branham and the other women and girl convicts had the same unpleasant treatment.

Out in the harbour they could see a fleet of eleven ships being made ready. This was the first fleet to take convicts to Botany Bay in New South Wales. Labourers were loading the ships with all the things that would be needed to start a new colony.

The eleven ships in the fleet were tiny. Modern ferries in Sydney Harbour, Portsmouth or Liverpool are bigger. Some of the ships took only food and equipment, and the rest each had about 150 people on board.

Mary Branham was rowed out to the *Lady Penrhyn* and chained up below decks. John Hudson was chained in the *Friendship*. Imagine what you would have felt like, with your ankles tied by a short chain to the inside of a dark, dank ship!

There were over 750 convicts, with marine soldiers to guard them, marines' families, and the sailors. Some convicts were allowed to take their families with them too. Some of the children were eight or nine years old. Others were even younger.

In all, nearly 1500 people sailed to Australia on 13 May 1787, under the command of Captain Arthur Phillip.

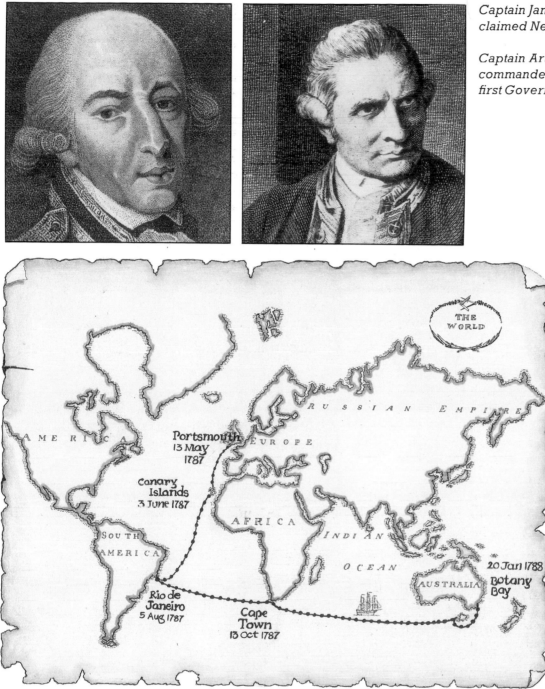

Captain James Cook (far left) who claimed New South Wales for Britain

Captain Arthur Phillip (left), commander of the First Fleet and first Governor of New South Wales

Some of the things taken by the First Fleet:
1 portable canvas house (for Governor Phillip)
18 turkeys
87 chickens
4 cows
1 bull
44 sheep
5 rabbits
589 women's petticoats
600 pounds of coarse sugar
1 dozen tin saucepans
1 printing press
1 set of candle-making equipment
1 bible
1 prayerbook
800 sets of bedding
5,440 drawers (*underwear*)
448 barrels of flour
60 bushels of seed wheat
1 piano
apple, pear, oak, fig and myrtle trees
300 gallons of brandy
10 pairs of handcuffs
8000 fish hooks
700 iron shovels
747,000 nails
12 ploughs
6 butcher's knives
60 padlocks
700 wooden platters
10,000 bricks
(*and much more*)

The storms were terrible, tossing the little ships up and down, and making everyone, including John Hudson and Mary Branham, sick, cold and miserable. The only good thing was that their chains were taken off after the first week. The journey took eight months. To John and Mary it seemed endless! Over forty people died and seven babies were born on the voyage.

At long last they arrived at Botany Bay. It was a disappointment. They soon saw there was hardly any fresh water and it wouldn't be a good place for farming.

Exploring north, a small party of marines came across Port Jackson. They decided this was the place to start the new colony.

> 'We got into Port Jackson early in the afternoon, and had the satisfaction of finding the finest harbour in the world, in which a thousand ships may ride in the most perfect security.'
> *Captain Phillip*

Captain Phillip named the new landing place Sydney Cove. This was to honour Lord Sydney, who had ordered the Fleet to be sent.

So, the Fleet dropped anchor for the last time on 26 January 1788, a hot summer's day. On the same day, a marine's wife, Elizabeth Whittle, gave birth to the first European child to be born in Sydney.

For the first few days everyone was very busy. The animals and stores were unloaded and the tents put up. John and Mary and the other convicts were used as labourers. They dug some of the land and planted seeds.

Watching from the bushes were the Koories.

ST. MARY'S COLLEGE
FALLS ROAD, BELFAST 12.

The First
SYDNEYSIDERS

John and Mary thought Sydney Cove was a very scary place. Everything looked and smelt and sounded strange. The bugs, moths and spiders were enormous and no one knew which ones were harmless. When they heard kookaburras, they thought madmen were laughing in the trees. Were there large, dangerous animals further inland?

Everyone huddled in their tents on the rocky sandstone edge of the cove. They called the place The Rocks. Wouldn't those first Sydneysiders have been surprised if they could have seen Caraher's Lane or The Rocks today? (If you turn back to page 12, and then to pages 2 and 3, you can do your own time-travelling.)

Things began to go wrong from the start. The convicts didn't know much about farming, and many of them were old and sick. Even good farmers would have found it hard. Australia's weather is harsh, the soil is dry and rocky, and there isn't much rain.

The seeds brought from England did not grow. Because there were so many to feed, the fish supplies ran out. The animals they had brought wandered off into the bush, where they were eaten by wild dingoes.

The people of the First Fleet nearly starved. Captain Phillip had to ration food equally between marines and convicts. When six marines were caught stealing food, they were punished just as if they were convicts – they were hanged.

The Koories often helped the newcomers. They showed them which plants, lizards and insects were safe to eat. But because they were so different, there were often misunderstandings between the settlers and the Koories. These led to clashes, and people were killed on both sides.

But death came to the Koories by accident as well. They caught diseases like colds, measles and smallpox from the settlers. Because these diseases had not existed in Australia before, the Koories were not immune to them. Many thousands died in a very few years after the British arrived.

Convicts in Australia

The convicts exchanged a hard way of life in Britain for a hard way of life in Australia. If they escaped, they usually did not live long. Men convicts were often kept chained together. These 'chain gangs' were forced to break-up rocks with sledgehammers. With the stones, they built the first roads. Women and child convicts were 'assigned'. They had to work as servants for the marines, the Governor, or the free settlers who began to come to New South Wales. Men could be assigned as labourers.

If you were a convict and you broke the law, or failed to work, you faced horrifying punishments. You might be locked up in a very small cell or lashed with a whip called the 'cat-o'-nine-tails'.

'I was only fourteen years old. There were only eight houses in the colony then. Myself and eighteen others laid in a hollow tree for seventeen weeks, and cooked out of a kettle with a wooden bottom. We used to stick it in the ground, and make a fire round it. I was chained seven weeks on my back for being out getting herbs.'

Child convict

GOOD CONDUCT REWARDS

Ticket-of-leave: The convict was allowed to work for himself or choose who to work for.
Pardons: The convict was let off some or all of his sentence.

CONVICT PUNISHMENTS

John Orr, a boy, twelve lashes for neglect of duty. He cried out very much.

John Green, for trying to escape, fifty lashes. Appeared to suffer much, bled freely, and fainted after the punishment.

Of course life was hard for the settlers as well, and there appears to have been little difference between them and the convicts.

As time went by, new convict settlements were started on the east coast of Australia, on Norfolk Island, and later in Perth. In Tasmania, convicts were harnessed to ploughs, and made to break up the stony soil, while the farmers used whips 'to encourage them', just as if they were animals.

Young settlers

Young convicts

Chain gang

Although their life was hard, the convicts had one ray of hope. When their sentence was finished, usually after seven years, they were freed, or emancipated. These 'emancipists' could then take up a grant of land from the government and become farmers. Many people in Australia today can trace their family back to an emancipated convict.

If you are an Australian Hudson, you could be descended from John Hudson. In 1791 he was given a free pardon. Later he was granted some land and was able to make a good living.

In 1813 Gregory Blaxland, William Lawson and William Charles Wentworth at last found a way over the Blue Mountains. Soon afterwards, chain gangs built a road. The explorer-settlers who travelled along it saw in front of them a huge and apparently empty plain. It was really the home of the Wiradjuri people, but to the settlers it meant land to be cleared for grazing sheep. It meant wealth.

Did You Know?

- The Blue Mountains got their name because they are covered in gum trees. The sun heats the eucalyptus oil in their leaves, and a blue haze hangs over them.

As more people came from Europe to farm sheep and cattle in Australia, they had to go further inland to find land that had not already been taken. These new settlers followed in the footsteps of the great explorers.

The settlers had to find ways of transporting wool and live animals hundreds of kilometres to sell in the cities on the coast. To begin with, this trade depended on rivers. Boats and paddle-steamers went up main rivers like the Murray. They took supplies to the settlers, and brought back wool and livestock.

Then, as the convicts built roads, long lines of bullocks could be seen pulling carts loaded high with wool. Sheep and cattle were driven along these roads to the cities, to be killed for meat. Roads were followed by railways during the 1850s and 1860s.

Burke and Wills and the Dig Tree

Of all the many Australian explorers, the story of Burke and Wills is the most tragic. Fifteen men set out from Melbourne in August 1860 to do what no other Europeans had done – to cross the continent from south to north. They faced the dry deserts of central Australia – the outback.

After three months they had gone a third of the way, and set up a supply base at Cooper's Creek. Burke, Wills, King, and Gray went on. In February 1861, they reached the Gulf of Carpentaria on the north coast. But then they faced a terrible struggle to get back. On the way Gray died in his sleep. At last, worn out after walking 2,500 kilometres, the other three got back to Cooper's Creek on 21 April. It was deserted.

As they looked round, they found the ashes of the fire were still warm. A message carved on a tree told them to dig one metre to the north-west. Buried in a box was the message, '21 April. The depot party leaves this camp today to return to the River Darling . . .' They had missed the main party by only a few hours.

Burke, Wills and King left Cooper's Creek to find help 240 kilometres away. The journey would take several days, and they soon found they were too weak. Tired and depressed, they struggled back to the Dig Tree again.

King accepted help from some Aboriginal People, and six months later a search party found him still alive. But the journey had been too much for Burke and Wills. After the ordeal of crossing some of the cruellest land in the world, the two explorers had died.

Large parts of Australia are desert, or semi-desert, and so some settlers imported camels. Many of the camel trains were brought with their drivers from Afghanistan.

Did You Know?
- From Perth to Sydney is 3,300 kilometres.
- From Darwin to Melbourne is 2,700 kilometres.
- Australia is approximately twenty-four times the size of the British Isles.

Because Australia is so big, and travel takes a long time, a telegraph wire was laid from Darwin to Alice Springs, and then to Adelaide. At last, people could send messages across the continent. Nowadays, of course, you can make a telephone call anywhere in Australia, and talk from Britain to Australia. Try to imagine how cut off families must have felt in the days when a letter from Britain to Australia could take up to nine months to arrive.

It's important to remember that long before roads and railways, the Aboriginal People walked the Dreaming Tracks across the whole continent (see page 34). They called meetings of tribal representatives, and traded between tribes.

Even today, people in the bush and outback can live hundreds of kilometres apart. But they keep in contact by telephones and two-way radios. People think nothing of driving several hundred kilometres to go to a rodeo, a cricket match, or to see friends and relations. Imagine how you would feel if you couldn't just walk round to see your friends when you wanted to!

A record load – 150 bales of wool weighing 17,600kg

29

SHEEP

Early on, John and Elizabeth Macarthur introduced merinos. These sheep are specially bred for a hot climate, and as well as making Macarthur's fortune they made certain that Australia would become an important wool-producer.

Wilpoorinna, where Adam and Sarah Litchfield live, is 100 kilometres across, with thousands of sheep. Its Aboriginal name means ' a place on the flat' – and it *is* flat!

If you went there, you might not even know you were on a sheep station, because you can't usually see any sheep! Fifty years ago Adam's grandfather went out on horseback to round them up. Nowadays, you muster by motorbike.

> 'This is a Peewee Fifty, a little motorbike. I use it to check the water, and every mustering season to muster sheep. Sometimes Sarah rides this and I drive the Toyota.'
> *Adam*

Merino ram

Shearing so many sheep is an immense job. Originally blade shears were used, but shearers have now changed to electric clippers. The teams travel round the country going from one sheep station to the next.

For a long time, wool-growing was Australia's main industry. People used to say that Australia lived 'off the sheep's back'.

In the 200 years since the First Fleet brought five rabbits to Australia, they have multiplied to many millions. They are now a real pest. Everyone on a station, including the kids, goes rabbit-shooting.

Did You Know?

- A sheep farm is called a sheep station in Australia.
- There are ten times more sheep than people in Australia.

Willpoorinna means Place on the Flat, that is why it is So flat. We have 16 shearers. It takes 10 days to shear 6,500 sheep. Each shearer shears approximate 120 sheep a day. It is hard to do school work when there is so much noise.

Love Adam

Squatters and Aboriginal People

Most of the early wool-growers were squatters (see page 10). In Australia, they were breaking the law, but there were so many of them that in the end the State governments had to accept that the land belonged to the squatters. This was a disaster for the Aboriginal People.

They thought the sheep were a new and plentiful food supply, so they hunted them. After all, the squatters hunted kangaroos and emus just like they did. The idea that people could own animals was unbelievable to Aboriginal People.

The squatters, on the other hand, were very clear about ownership. They knew that according to British law, anyone who stole a sheep could be hanged. Because the police might be hundreds of kilometres away, the squatters took the law into their own hands, hunting and killing the Aboriginal People. It didn't occur to them that they might have different laws.

It was the same with the land. The Aboriginal People believed that land could not belong to a person because it was sacred. You could travel over it, hunt on it, make fires on it. But you had to look after your tribe's land, and you couldn't own it personally (and nor could anyone else.) You couldn't sell it or give it away because it wasn't yours to give.

Aboriginals charged with spearing cattle in 1901

The squatters fenced off land, and anyone who came on 'their property' was a trespasser. So the places where the Aboriginal People could live became fewer and fewer. Some found work on sheep stations. Many more died from European diseases, or were simply killed off for being in the way of the new settlers. By 1900 their numbers had fallen by over three-quarters.

An Aboriginal stockman

Some settlers felt it was their duty to help the Aboriginal People. They took the children away from their tribes and taught them to read and write, to sing hymns, and to take part in physical education. All of this would have been very useful if the Aboriginal People had wanted to become like the British settlers, but most of them wanted to stay as they were.

'The missionaries took us into the dormitory at the age of three years old and there we had to learn to speak like our mission ladies. We were not allowed to talk lingo [our language], because we might learn our legends and things like that, you see. But my mother taught me some of our culture. She knew all the history of the different tribes.'
Mapoon Aboriginal

The Dreaming

'Ngangatja apu wiya, ngayuku tjamu' – 'This is not a rock, it is my grandfather.' *Pitjantjatjara People*

The Dreaming is the most important thing the Aboriginal People believe in. It holds the living, those who have died, and the landscape, together in one complete world.

The elders tell Gordon, Crystal and Sally, the young Nyoongahs, all about the Dreaming.

'When we look at the land, we don't see just rocks and scrub, we see the past and all the people who have been in that place. We know their stories, the stories of the place.

'For us the landscape is living. In the beginning, the Dreamtime, beings travelled from place to place in the form of humans, animals and plants. They did all kinds of strange deeds. When they stopped in their travelling, they became mountains, rivers, deserts, plains and trees, and these are what we see today.

'We say all these places are reminders of what links the land to the Dreaming. We can take you to a rock or a tree that is our grandfather or grandmother. This is why the land is so sacred to us. It is our people, our mother.'

'An important part of our way of life is visiting the special pools, or rocks, or trees, where the spirits of our ancestors live. We call this "walking the Dreaming Tracks". There are many of them, all across Australia.

'Because the places on the Dreaming Track are sacred, we decorate the rocks with our art. Some of us must renew the painting as it fades, and others paint new on the old. Rock art is like layers in time.

'We paint the animals and birds in our lives. When we saw Europeans and their ships, we made a new layer on the rocks. Look at old hands-in-his-pocket! That's what white people look like. We notice them!'

Passing on traditions is very important to any civilisation. As we saw earlier on page 5, Aboriginal People teach their children how to make boomerangs and musical instruments, and how to dance and decorate themselves, as well as passing on the skills of living in the bush.

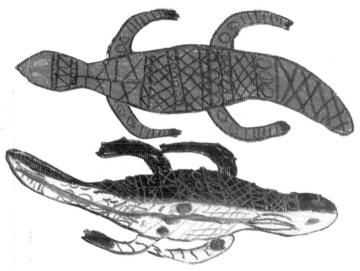

Nyoongah Learning
Infants:

Learn the names and positions of the stars.

Learn to use your eyes to follow a single ant.

From ten years old:

Learn to endure pain.

Learn who are your kin and who you can marry.

Learn to get all your own food.

Ken Colbung teaches the Nyoongah kids:
'Here in front of us, it's called a wattle tree. Now in the bark you'll find that they get what we call a bardie or a witchetty grub. You can easily notice it by bits of sawdust at the bottom of the hole. Also in there you'll see some gluey stuff. We call it manna gum, and that gum is always eaten by children going along . . . The wood is used for making shields, and when you get the tall thin ones, you can make spears from them . . . And these boughs make quite good digging sticks for women . . . So we get quite a bit besides having shade.'

Playing a didgeridoo

The Rainbow Serpent

For Aboriginal People, showing and telling other people is more important than writing instructions or books. If you were a young Aboriginal person you would hear many stories.

Vivian Walker, an Aboriginal writer, tells you this story of the Dreamtime. If you want to know what it's like to be a young Aboriginal, get someone to tell you the story. Or tell it yourself in your own words, perhaps to a younger brother, sister or friend.

The Beginning of Life

Once, the sleeping earth was flat, dark and cold. No creature stirred. There were no hills and valleys, no trees or rivers.

In the centre of Australia, far beneath the surface of the earth, the Rainbow Serpent, Mother of Life, grew restless in her sleep. It was time for her to give birth to the children in her belly – all the animal tribes.

Slowly, she uncurled from her cramped sleeping place and began to burrow her way to the surface. But something stopped her. A great rock was in her way. For many many moons the Mother of Life pushed and pushed the boulder up. Inch by inch it moved until one day, it burst on to the surface. The Rainbow Serpent pushed it aside and looked around at the desolate landscape. She needed to rest from her labour. Before she set off on her wanderings, she turned to look at the rock which had gained its freedom like a baby, and she said: 'You are my first-born, you will be called Uluru.'

Her travels took her far and wide across the land. When she grew tired, she curled herself into a circle to sleep and regain her strength. When she awoke, she looked back and saw the deep winding tracks where she had travelled. Where she had slept, great hollows had been left, looking out of place on the flat plains.

Now she felt the staggering pain of her babies crying to be free. It was time to return to Uluru. When she got back to the place of her first-born, she made herself ready. She called to the frog tribes inside her to come out. They had been sleeping for many many seasons and moved slowly, heavy with the water they had stored in their stomachs for the long hibernation before their birth. They shook their lazy heads. They did not want to give up their precious water but the wise mother tickled their stomachs. When they laughed, the water flowed in torrents from their mouths to fill the tracks of the Rainbow Serpent's wanderings, to make lakes and rivers, oceans and streams.

Suddenly, the scene was still. A far rumbling could be heard, and like a burst of laughter, grass began to grow, trees sprang up and flowers bloomed. Life had begun on earth. All the animal tribes, the kangaroo, the emu, the platypus and kookaburra flowed from the Rainbow Serpent to join their frog brothers. They flew and hopped, scurried and slithered all over the land and sky. They were happy on the earth.

Now each animal stayed with his brothers and sisters, and hunted and played in harmony. The galah tribe preferred to live in the treetops and the snake tribe hunted between the rocks and trees. Each tribe knew that this was the law of the Rainbow Serpent.

The wise old woman looked at her happy children and said: 'There is food for all. Each tribe will be a totem. Let no one eat of his own totem for there is food for all. Those who keep this law, I will reward with human life. You and your children's children shall roam this land in happiness, hunting and playing forever. Those who disobey, I will punish and turn to stone, to sit in gloom until the end of time.'

And so it was. Those who broke the Rainbow Serpent's laws, she turned to mountains, hills and stones. They were left to sit while their brothers and sisters played and hunted at their feet. To those who kept the laws, she gave a human form and each human tribe kept as their totem the animal they had once been.

The tribes know themselves by their totems and a kangaroo man does not eat his brother, the kangaroo. In this way the Mother of Life, the Rainbow Serpent, makes sure that there is always food for all her children.

ULURU

Uluru is a site that is very sacred to the Aboriginal People. On older maps Uluru is still called Ayers Rock. It is a very unusual formation because it is a monolith, a single huge rock, sticking up out of a flat plain. Many tourists go and see it, and walk the 9 kilometres all around its base. Some of them climb up its steep sides.

The guides only take tourists to certain parts of Uluru. This is because it is sacred to the Anangu. There are caves covered in rock art, and one of them is a special place where Anangu women go to give birth. They have gone to that same place for thousands of years.

Recently, Aboriginal People have been trying to get the Australian government to give them some of their land back. Ayers Rock was handed over on 26 October 1985 and became Uluru once again.

At Ayers Rock
Here, I sit in the hot sand
listening to bird sounds
and dingoes fight at night.
Here, around the camp-fire
talking is of old times.
Lyell Bowie, sixteen-year-old Nyoongah

MINING

Australia is rich in coal and iron ore, as well as many other rare and valuable minerals such as diamonds, opals and uranium. They have to be mined and then sold overseas in order to pay for cars, trucks, televisions and washing-machines. If Australia had to rely on selling only wool and beef overseas, people's standard of living in the cities would be very much lower. Measured by money and goods, it would be a poorer country. The problem is that much of Australia's mineral wealth is found in those parts of the country which Aboriginal People believe are sacred. At first, people set up mines wherever they liked. Nowadays, Aboriginal People voice their views about the land more strongly.

> 'We feel very hurt when we see big holes dug in the ground. We think of our mother with a big cut in her body.'
> *Robert Bropho*

If you were a member of the House of Representatives, Australia's parliament, how would you weigh up the need for Australia to be prosperous, against the Aboriginal People's views?

GOLD...

The earliest mining in Australia was for gold. In 1851 the first real discoveries were made at Bathurst (just beyond the Blue Mountains), and Ballarat and Bendigo in Victoria. People heard the news and rushed from all over the world to make their fortune. The Gold Rush was on!

John Chandler was thirteen when he and his father joined the gold rush. He was amazed at the huge numbers of people streaming towards the goldfields – men on horseback, families on foot, groups in bullock carts piled with equipment, and surprisingly, large numbers of Chinese talking in a language John had never heard before.

He was very excited when they climbed over a ridge and saw below them the tents of Golden Point.

John and his father set up their own camp and John went off to watch the prospectors digging and panning for gold. As he looked around he saw many families like his own. Because they were desperate to make a fortune, even the children had to work.

COPY CAT FROM BALLARAT
FIND SOME GOLD AND YOU'LL GET FAT!

John wanted some of those bright shiny specks of metal for himself, and he soon learnt how to pan for gold. But the first prospectors to get to Golden Point had already staked the best claims. Like so many others, John and his father were unlucky. They still managed to make a living though, by carting supplies to the goldfields.

Bernard Holtermann was one of a group of gold-diggers who worked for several years, finding just enough to keep going. Several of his mates gave up, but the others kept digging. Imagine how they felt when, in October 1872, they found a whole reef of gold! Chipping away with their pickaxes, they managed to get out an enormous lump!

Holtermann's nugget was the largest ever found, a mixture of slate and gold. When it was crushed, they extracted 99.8 kilograms of pure gold. That's the weight of three or four kids, and today, it would be worth a million pounds, or over two million Australian dollars.

In parts of Australia, you can still be lucky and pick up a nugget of gold in a field – just like this boy did!

How to pan for gold

1 First find a stream running through a goldfield . . .
2 Dig out the rocky earth 3 Place a small amount of earth in the bottom of a pan. (You could use a frying-pan.) Pour a little water in, swirl it round and let it trickle over the edge, carrying away the dirt and small stones. 4 Gold (which is a very heavy metal) gets left behind, but usually only in tiny quantities.
5 A faster way is with a wooden panning machine like the ones in the pictures!

...and BUSHRANGERS!

Gus Wernicke was fifteen when he was shot dead. He was one of Captain Moonlite's gang of bushrangers. Bushrangers are like highwaymen or outlaws in Britain.

Quite a few of Australia's first bushrangers were escaped convicts. They must have had a hard life until gold was found. Then, suddenly, there were coaches with prospectors carrying their new-found wealth back to the banks in the towns and cities. 'Why don't we take their pouches of nuggets?' said Gus and the rest of the gang. 'Once they're in our pockets, no one can prove who the original owner was.'

For a while, the bushrangers did well out of gold, but like Gus and the Moonlite gang, many were shot by the police.

The best-known bushranger is Ned Kelly. His family were poor because his father, an ex-convict, had died. Ned's brother Dan stole horses, and one day when Ned was away, Constable Fitzpatrick came to arrest Dan. Dan and his mother put up a fight and Fitzpatrick was wounded. Dan escaped but Ellen Kelly was sent to jail for three years.

The two angry brothers went to live in the bush and were soon joined by their friends Joe Byrne and Steve Hart. Troopers (or policemen) were sent to arrest the gang, there was a fight at Stringybark Creek, and three troopers were killed.

V.

£8000
ROBBERY

WHEREAS EDWARD KELLY, DAN... been declared OUTLAWS in the Co... the aforesaid men with the WILF... Colony of VICTORIA, and whereas the above... divers felonies in the Colony of NEW SOUTH... ROBINSON, the GOVERNOR, do, by this... hereby notify that a REWARD of £4,00... WALES, and one fourth by certain Bank... Offenders, or a reward of £1000 for the a... reward, a similar REWARD of £400... notify that the said REWARD will... shall lead to the apprehension of the offe... effect such apprehension or assist therea...

Dated 15th February,

The Kelly Gang robbed a bank, held up a police station and took over the town of Jerilderie for two days! They became a legend, and over ten months the reward for their capture grew from £200 to £8000, a huge sum of money in those days. (Equal to about a million pounds today, or over two million Australian dollars.)

The gang knew that there would be a shoot-out, so they made armour for themselves out of iron ploughshares. When the police arrived, Ned advanced on them like a strange iron-clad apparition.

Only when the police fired at his legs were they able to stop Ned. At the age of 25, he was taken to Melbourne, tried, found guilty and hanged. But Ned Kelly's spirit of independence caught the imagination of Australians and his legend lives on.

Ned Kelly's last words on the scaffold:
'Ah well, I suppose it has come to this . . . Such is life!'

R.

REWARD

d MURDER.

LLY, STEPHEN HART and JOSEPH BYRNE have
. and whereas warrants have been issued charging
Victoria, and whereas SCANLON, Police Constable of the
RDER of MICHAEL SCANLON, and have recently committed
fenders are STILL at LARGE, and have recently committed
S; Now, therefore, I, SIR HERCULES GEORGE ROBERT
lamation issued with the advice of the Executive Council,
amation issued by the Government of NEW SOUTH
e paid, three-fourths by the apprehension of the above-named Four
in the Colony, for the apprehension ADDITION to the above
n of any one of them; and that, in ADDITION to the above
en offered by the Government of VICTORIA, and I further
bly apportioned between any persons giving information which
, any members of the police force or other persons who may actually

(Signed) HENRY PARKES,
Colonial Secretary, New South Wales.

(Signed) BRYAN O'LOGHLEN,
Attorney General, Victoria.

45

For many years, life in the bush was very hard. These children probably helped their Dad build this rough wooden hut. They had to use whatever came to hand. To make a floor, they trod down the dirt. They were plagued by flies and mosquitoes all the time (and still would be nowadays), but these must have seemed quite homely compared with the other strange insects! Moths and spiders, grubs and beetles, are all bigger and scarier than in Britain. There are poisonous spiders, scorpions and snakes.

Families still dressed as if they were in Britain. Yet the temperature could easily be 30 or 35 degrees Celsius. The kids probably hated being dressed like this, but for their mums and dads it was a way of remembering their old life.

'I think my dear mother suffered from homesickness in those days. We would go into the bush a little way, and in her sweet musical voice she would sing to me sad little songs about people far from home.'

Margaret Mickle, Tasmania

46

If you had an accident, your family had to know what to do. Otherwise the journey to a doctor might take days on horseback.

The Flying Doctor

If you have an accident these days, you can call the Flying Doctor. If he can't fix you on the spot, you'll get a ride in his light aircraft back to a hospital. Worth having your appendix out for, isn't it? – well almost!

> 'There was a small girl who lived close to us who cut her leg badly on a broken bottle and no matter what they did they couldn't stop the bleeding. As a last resort, they plastered her leg with flour.'
>
> *G. Facey*, Victoria

Not surprisingly, many children died young. Mothers found it hard to keep babies alive in the dirt and heat. If you lived to grow up in Australia, you were tough. For those who didn't survive, there were no graveyards, just a clearing in the bush and a wooden cross.

Perhaps some of the immigrants wondered whether it was all worth it. Was the life so much better than life in the slums?

Did You Know?

- Australia has two deadly spiders, the red-back and the funnel-web.
- A red-back spider bite can kill children.
- A funnel-web spider bite can kill you in 15 minutes. (90 minutes if you are grown up.)

(Like snakes, spiders are more scared of you than you are of them, and will try to keep out of your way. Effective anti-venoms to cure their bites are now available.)

These spiders are life-size and they're often even bigger!

Living in the Towns

Some businessmen grew very rich and wanted grand houses. Most Australian houses have verandahs, but not running round like these!

The more people settled in Australia, the more there was a need for shops and businesses. What can you see The Little Wonder store selling? What do you imagine you could have bought there?

Verandahs are not just decorative – they are also very practical. For instance, in summer you can sleep on the verandah.

> 'It's a shelter – saves you getting wet when you're eating or having a party outside. If it's too hot, it stops the sun. If you're eating something icy, it stops it melting too quick. A verandah's just like a sun-protector.'
>
> *Nellie and Gordon,* Wanneroo, Perth

The way people lived in towns like Tamworth in the early 1900s would have seemed luxurious to the early settlers. You wouldn't have found a wide street and houses with verandahs like this anywhere in Britain in 1900. But you can still see them in Australia today.

The Pope Family

Kylie and Stephen live in Ryde, a northern suburb of Sydney. They can trace their family right back to the time when Ryde was a little town. In 1838, George Pope, his wife Jane, and their children first came to Sydney. Kylie and Stephen are their great-great-great-great-grandchildren! George and Jane are buried in Ryde Cemetery.

In the Archives Office of New South Wales, you can see records of the Popes' arrival. They were one of the many families who emigrated from Britain to Australia.

The Popes' story turned into a happy one eventually. George and Jane started making shoes again, and eight years later George became Ryde's postmaster.

George Pope was a shoemaker in the Isle of Wight, and Jane was a shoebinder. When their little shop failed to get enough customers, the family had to go into the Workhouse. This was a large grim building. Here, the family was split up and they had to work hard in return for bed, shelter and just enough to eat.

George's eldest son, George Miller Pope, was nine years old when he arrived in Ryde. He grew up to become an important man and there is even a street named after him.

To emigrate, the Popes needed a grant of money, and for two years they applied to the Workhouse Guardians. At last they were lucky, and were given a grant of £3 in money and clothing, and tickets for the voyage on the *William Metcalfe*.

CAUTION.

THE Commander of the Ship WILLIAM METCALFE hereby informs the Public that he will not be responsible for any Debts which the Crew of his Vessel may contract.

Sydney, 7th October, 1834.

George Miller Pope built the little stone court-house that still stands near the church and became clerk of court.

BUSHFIRES

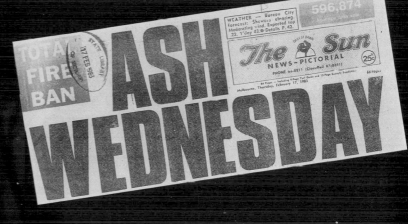

TOTAL FIRE BAN

WEATHER — Bureau City
Forecast: Showers clearing.
Moderating wind. Expected top
22. Y'day 43. Details P. 42.

596,874

The Sun
NEWS - PICTORIAL

25c

PHONE 64-0351 (Classified 41-0351)

Melbourne, Thursday, February 17, 1983

ASH WEDNESDAY

Did You Know?

- Bushfires spread quickly through the oily gum trees and dry bush. One of the worst bushfires in recent times was on Ash Wednesday 1983, in Victoria and South Australia. A wall of flame spread 1,200 kilometres across the states, leaping roads and threatening towns. A fire on that scale in Europe would spread from London to Vienna in Austria.
- In 1974 and 1975 bushfires burnt 1.25 million square kilometres – a sixth of Australia!

DUST STORMS

The strong winds whip up Australia's red soil to make rolling clouds of fine dusty sand. In a very short time, everything looks as though it has been spray-painted from above.

'It got really windy – all this sand came up, and all this paper, and the wind picked up all the chairs that we've got around the pool and all the blankets, and threw them up on the roof of the house. Blew the towels right down the end of the road!'

Tammy and Ossie Balzer

Dust storm approaches Melbourne

CYCLONES

DARWIN WIPED OUT

THE TOLL:
49 DEAD
30,000 HOMELESS

The Sun
NEWS-PICTORIAL

Killer cyclone flattens a city

Did You Know?

- A cyclone is a tropical storm with heavy rain and very strong winds. The winds rush round like water in a whirlpool, sometimes at over 200 kilometres per hour.

'The clouds were black. The house was shaking with thunder. The cyclone was here and I was terrified so I ran to Mum. We all ran to the bathroom because it was small. Late at night the lounge room ceiling fell in. All the wind came in and I was freezing cold. The next morning the cyclone had gone. I went to the front door and it creaked. Dad came out the creaky door and helped me clean up.'

Kellie Rossiter (aged 8), South Hedland

FLOODS

Darwin hit by Cyclone Tracy, 1974

'Quite often in summertime we can have a temperature of 40 degrees Celsius and wake up in the morning like today – clear blue sky. Then, in the middle of the afternoon, you start getting a few clouds building up and by 5 o'clock you're knee-deep in water from a terrible downpour.'

Ken Walker, Western Australia

When your street is under water, you need a new way of getting around – like these kids in Brisbane

CYCLONE WARNINGS

STAGE BLUE

- A cyclone may affect your area within 48 hours. Check your preparation.
- Fit cyclone screens.

STAGE YELLOW

- The cyclone will be in your area in 12 hours.
- Store or secure loose materials.
- Check cyclone screens are secure.
- Top up vehicle fuel tanks,
- Fill emergency water containers.

STAGE RED

- Cyclone about to reach you!
- Stay in your home.
- Put pets in safe shelters.
- Park vehicles in gear.
- If you are caught outside, lie down and crawl to shelter.
- Listen to the radio for up-to-date instructions.

Australian animals

To emigrants, some Australian animals must have seemed very strange. See if you can match the name to the animal. (Answers below.)

Koala, Gallah, Kookaburra, Dingo, Frangipani, Wombat Duck-billed platypus, Crocodile, Emu, Kangaroo, King parrot, Rosella.

Answers 1 Koala, 2 Galah, 3 Kookaburra, 4 Dingo (wild dog), 5 Frangipani, 6 Duck-bi

Australians at WAR

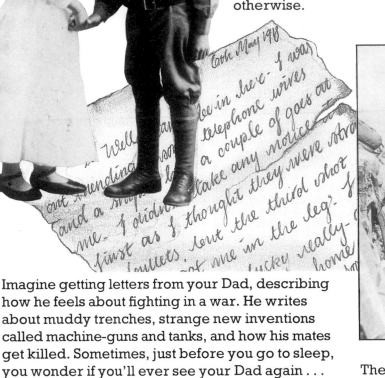

The First World War: 1914–1918

These two children look very proud to be dressed up as an Anzac soldier and a Red Cross nurse. He's wearing a 'digger's' hat. There was a reason for tying up the brim. When a soldier put his rifle on his shoulder for marching he'd knock his hat off otherwise.

Many children's fathers went off to fight in the First World War. In those days Australians still called Britain the 'home country'. So when Britain went to war with Germany, it seemed natural to send soldiers in support. New Zealand joined in as well and the troops were called the Australian and New Zealand Army Corps – the ANZACS.

Imagine getting letters from your Dad, describing how he feels about fighting in a war. He writes about muddy trenches, strange new inventions called machine-guns and tanks, and how his mates get killed. Sometimes, just before you go to sleep, you wonder if you'll ever see your Dad again . . .

There are months between his letters. At last, on 11 November 1918 your Mum shows you a newspaper headline. The war is over! But your Dad still has to get home.

Then, two or three months later, there's a telegram. Suddenly you and your Mum have to get busy. You get out the flags and decorate the front of the house. At long last, you see a familiar figure walking down the road.
Dad . . .!

The Second World War 1939–1945

The Second World War was much closer to home for Australians. Japanese soldiers took over many Pacific islands, including New Guinea, Australia's nearest northern neighbour.

If you had been at school during the war, you'd have taken part in air-raid drills. This meant standing up with your first-aid kit round your shoulders, and plugging your ears up so that a bomb-blast wouldn't make you permanently deaf.

Kids in Darwin and other northern Australian towns needed their air-raid drill because of Japanese attacks. In Sydney, midget submarines entered the harbour and torpedoed a ship.

All schoolchildren had to help in the war by collecting silver paper, newspapers, old car tyres and scrap metal. All of this could be recycled – saved up and used again.

Once more, fathers had to go and fight, but in this war, women took part as well, although they weren't allowed to serve overseas. You might have had a sister or an aunt who joined the Women's Auxiliary Australian Air Force (the WAAF), the Australian Women's Army Service (the AWAS), or the Women's Royal Australian Naval Service (the WRANS).

Every Australian got a ration book which had pages full of coupons, rather like stamps. When you went shopping you had to hand over coupons as well as money. No matter how much money you had, if you used up all the week's sweet coupons, you got no more lollies!

At last you'd see Anzacs and American troops boarding ships at Brisbane and Rockhampton. They were going to fight the Japanese in New Guinea and the other islands, as a first step to ending the Pacific war.

After the war, many people came to Australia. They often came from homes that had been destroyed by war.

57

z in the Sky

Australia is so big that, to start with, it was a number of separate colonies. Later they became states with their own flags. Dalia and Nikki live in New South Wales, Gordon, Crystal and Sally in Western Australia, Adam and Sarah in South Australia.

But they are all Australians! This is because in 1901 the states agreed to have one overall (federal) government, and a flag for the whole of Australia. Australia is part of the British Commonwealth and Queen Elizabeth II is Queen of Australia too.

Did You Know?

● Melbourne and Sydney, the two biggest cities, couldn't agree which should be the capital of Australia, so a brand-new capital was built, Canberra.

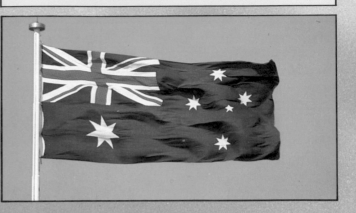

At night in Australia, the sky looks quite different from the way it looks in Britain. You're looking out into the universe in a different direction! The best-known star formation is the Southern Cross – the stars on the Australian flag.

Look up in the daytime, and you may see wattle blossom. This is Australia's national flower and its green and gold are Australia's national colours.

z in your Pocket

Dip your hand in your pocket and what have you got? If you're lucky, a pocketful of dollars? (Or maybe a handful of cents.)
Dollars and cents are the money that Dalia and Nikki, Adam and Sarah, Gordon, Crystal and Sally use. One hundred cents make a dollar, and there are between 2 and 2.5 Australian dollars to the British pound. Both British and local money were in use in the early days. John and Mary must have found this complicated. Money made in Australia was called 'currency' while British money was called 'sterling'.

Did You Know?

● Currency gave its name to children born in the colony. They were 'Currency Lads and Lasses', unlike the 'sterling' immigrants.

Oz and the Bomb

The Southern Cross is on the PND symbol as well as the Australian flag. People for Nuclear Disarmament is like CND in Britain. They want to persuade people to get rid of the nuclear bomb because it's so destructive and because of its dangerous radiation. The opposite argument is that if your country has nuclear bombs, other countries will be too frightened to attack you.

In the 1950s the British government tested nuclear bombs at Maralinga in the Great Victoria Desert – an area Aboriginal People move through. The bombs threw up lots of soil, turning it into radioactive dust. This fallout came down over large areas of the desert, and unless it is cleaned up, the desert will be dangerous to people, animals and plants, for centuries to come.

Oz and the Land

These days, many Aboriginal People live in poor housing, often without work. They want to get back some of their traditional land. They use petitions and marches to voice their views about Land Rights.

> 'We're not saying, ''All you white people take your belongings and sail home again.'' We're saying, ''We want you to share with us, the same as we shared with you when you came here.'''
> *Robert Bropho*

Some people see the arrival of the British in 1788 as a kind of invasion.

Did You Know?

- The Aboriginal Flag is black for the people, red for the land and yellow for the sun.

 at School

Most British kids would love to swap their school for an Australian one. Schools like Dalia's and Nikki's often have classes at the beach! There aren't many schools in Britain where you tan as you learn!

Their school is like many in Australia. There are forty-nine nationalities. Dalia and Nikki are friends with kids whose parents are Italian, Lebanese, Japanese and Filipino.

Kids from many countries helped make this mural at Bondi Beach School

Sally at the Nyoongah school

Sarah in the Wilpoorinna schoolroom

Adam and Sarah, though, have the School of the Air. Because the nearest school is hundreds of kilometres away, they go to their schoolroom at Wilpoorinna homestead. Inside, there's a two-way radio, and they can tune in to hear their teacher giving a lesson. There are three or four other children in each 'class', spread over thousands of square kilometres. They're all given work over the radio. It might be reading or writing, but it could just as well be a science experiment. If you have a question, don't put your hand up – get on the radio!

You can still make friends through School of the Air because you can use the radio to talk to the other kids in your 'class'. There are summer camps as well, when you have the fun of finding faces to fit the voices.

Long before School of the Air, bush schools looked like large squatters' huts. There were so many gaps letting in light that they didn't need any windows!

Can you write as neatly as this schoolgirl from the early 1900s?

Bush lesson – looking at a snakeskin

Kids at the Beach

If there's one place which sums Australia up, it's the beach. It's not just for holidays – it's part of a way of life.

Robert and David Campbell go to the same school as Dalia and Nikki. In summer they go down to the beach every single day, even after school. Well, nearly every day! They love surfing, whether it's on surfboards or boogie-boards.

'A surfboard – you can stand up on, and you've got the strap around your leg. A boogie-board is much smaller. It's got two fins that guide you and you put the strap around your hand. You don't paddle like you do on a surfboard, you lie on a boogie-board and kick with your flippers.' *Robert*

Robert and David are getting quite good in the surf with their boogie-boards, but that doesn't stop them from being dumped!

'Dumping is when you catch a big wave and you fall off the wave, and you get crushed up underneath. You fall off your boogie-board and it hits you on the head. That's being dumped – or you can call it – "barrelled".' *David*

All kids look like this – brightly coloured zinc cream protects your face from sunburn

Between eleven and three, slip under a tree.

Don't get BBQ'd in the bush.
For maximum protection against sunburn, skin damage and skin cancer, slip on a shirt, slop on sunscreen and slap on a hat.

The best sunscreen of all is absolutely free. So, when the sun is at its strongest, find a spot in the shade.

'When you go to the beach you've got to *slip* on a shirt, *slop* on some sunscreen and *slap* on a hat. Slip, slop, slap!' *Robert and Dalia*

Beaches in Australia are fun but Robert and David know they have hidden dangers. A tan is great but too much Australian sun can cause skin cancer when you're older. Some dangers are a bit nearer!

Robert and David have joined the Nippers, which is a junior lifesaving club. They learn about surf safety and lifesaving, and they take part in surf carnivals.

'A surf carnival is when all different lifesavers come from all different beaches and have a big competition. They do runs and swims, and they practice rescuing people.'

Robert

'In the middle of the beach, there's a big red bell in case any sharks come. And if the bell doesn't work, all these lifesavers will run out all over the beach, blow their whistles, and tell people to get out of the water. Then some of them just get in the boats and chase the shark back past the nets – because there's nets between both cliffs.'

Robert

'In England you go out and it's snowing outside. Up here we go outside and we're getting sunburnt.'

Ossie Balzer

If there is one time of the year when the difference between Britain and Australia shows most, it must be Christmas. Christmas in the middle of summer, with Christmas trees and Santa on the beach! Keep this picture in your mind as you fly back to Britain!

Oz-Pom Words and Phrases

A swaggie

Oz	Pom
arvo	*afternoon*
Aussie	*Australian*
Aussie Rules	*Australian Rules football*
banksia	*native Australian tree*
barbie	*barbecue*
beaut	*really good*
bewdy, mate	*wonderful!*
bludger	*skiver*
billy	*can for boiling water in*
boogie-board	*a board for body-surfing on*
brekky	*breakfast*
Brissie	*Brisbane*
chook	*chicken*
Chrissie	*Christmas*
cornies	*cornflakes*
daks	*trousers/slacks*
dam	*a man-made pond*
digger	*Australian soldier*
dingo	*Australian wild dog*
dinky-di	*genuine*
esky	*picnic box to keep things cool*
fish 'n' greasies	*fish and chips*
flake 'n' chips	*shark and chips*
galah	*Australian bird*
great galah	*stupid twit*
hang a U-ey	*do a U-turn*
he dobbed me in	*he told on me*
in the nuddy	*naked*
milk bar	*corner shop selling a bit of everything*
milko	*milkman*
mossie	*mosquito*
no worries	*fine!*
Oz	*Australia – the land down under!*
paddock	*field*
pav = pavlova	*large meringue filled with cream and fruit*
Pom/Pommie	*British person*
postie	*postman*
pressie	*present*
rellies	*relatives*
skite	*show-off*
stickybeak	*busybody/noseyparker*
stock	*livestock/farm animals*
sunnies	*sunglasses*
swaggie/swagman	*a wanderer or travelling bush worker who sleeps out in the open*
thongs	*flip-flops*
togs	*swimming costume*
tucker	*food*
ute	*utility truck*
vegemite	*Australian marmite*
vegies	*vegetables*
winnie	*sweatshirt*
yabbies	*edible crayfish living in dams and rivers*